Emily Post

Emily's Out and About Book

By Cindy Post Senning, Ed.D., and Peggy Post

Illustrated by Leo Landry

Collins

An Imprint of HarperCollinsPublishers

Emily's Out and About Book
Text copyright © 2009 by The Emily Post Institute, Inc.
Illustrations copyright © 2009 by Leo Landry
Manufactured in China.

Library of Congress Cataloging-in-Publication Data
Senning, Cindy Post.
    Emily's out and about book / by Cindy Post Senning, Ed.D, and Peggy Post ;
illustrated by Leo Landry. — 1st ed.
            p.   cm.
    Summary: On a trip around town with her mother, Emily demonstrates the
importance of having good manners.
    ISBN 978-0-06-111700-8 (trade bdg.) — ISBN 978-0-06-111701-5 (lib. bdg.)
    [1. Etiquette—Fiction.   2. Safety—Fiction.]   I. Post, Peggy, 1945–   II.
Landry, Leo, ill.   III. Title.
PZ7.S476Eq   2009   2008029286
[E]—dc22   CIP
                                                                  AC

Typography by Jeanne L. Hogle
09   10   11   12   13   SCP   10   9   8   7   6   5   4   3   2   1
❖
First Edition

Dedicated to toddlers everywhere
—C.P.S. and P.P.

For Cindy and Peggy
—L.L.

Emily has a busy day ahead of her.
She is going out and about with her mother.

Emily knows just what to do when she visits
different places and meets new people.

The first stop is the library.

She knows to use her quiet voice here,
even when she finds a book she really likes.

Next, Mom has a doctor's appointment.

Waiting isn't always easy!

But it gives Emily a chance to read her book.

There is a marketplace across the
street from the doctor's office.

Emily knows to wait for the green light, look both ways, and hold Mom's hand until they are safely across the street.

There are so many people! Emily stays
close to Mom so she won't get lost.

Emily stops to smell the roses.
The flowers are so pretty.

Emily knows to ask before she touches them.

Mom picks out a red top for Emily.
But Emily thinks the pink one is prettier.

"Could I have that one, please?" she says.
Mom thinks pink is pretty, too!

Emily and her mom will have
lunch before heading home.
Emily loves tacos.

She waits quietly in line and then
sits at her own table.

It's not easy to eat tacos neatly, but
Emily knows how to use her napkin.

Mom's friend Mrs. Jackson is having lunch, too.
Emily says hello and smiles at Mrs. Jackson.

Mrs. Jackson has a nice little dog. Emily knows to ask before she pets him.

Mrs. Jackson says Jonah is shy about meeting new people. Next time he will get to know Emily better.

Emily has had a busy day.

She is looking forward to going out
and about again soon.

But it is always good to be home!

Dear Parents,

Children are never too young to learn about manners. But at every age it is important for them to learn that manners are about more than a polite curtsey or bow. We want toddlers to understand that manners will help them get along well with people. For example, it is good manners to use a quiet voice when a loud voice will disturb others. Emily can help you teach your toddler to use a quiet voice in the library or in a doctor's waiting room. When you talk to your toddlers, you can add some of the other places they will use their quiet voices: in a church or in a shop, at preschool or at grandmother's house.

It is also good manners to share a nice greeting and a smile with people you meet. Mrs. Jackson feels *so* good when Emily gives her that big smile.

Please and *thank you* are called magic words for good reason. Emily's *please* when she asks her mother for the pink shirt instead of the red one shows the magic of that special word. Not only does Emily get her shirt in a lovely pink, but her mother feels good about the way it all happened. Look at her mother's big smile, too!

In addition to helping us get along with others, manners also bring order to our universe—whether it is the universe of a three-year-old or an adult. In the universe of the three-year-old, that order often means safety. For instance, it is polite to wait patiently for the light to turn green. It is polite to ask before patting a strange dog.

It is polite to hold on to your mother's hand when you are in a crowded store. As Emily reminds us in this story, all these manners can also be essential to safety.

Know your child so you can have reasonable expectations. Some toddlers can step right out and say hello with gusto. Other toddlers may be shy and hide behind your knee for another few months. They both can say hello and smile but each from his or her own place. And by the time they are six, they both should be able to add a handshake to their greeting. All the manners Emily demonstrates in this book are reasonable for most toddlers.

Children learn manners by practice and repetition. They forget easily, so when they are out and about, parents need to remind them often to use good manners. If these lessons are a litany of *no* and *don't*, children will begin to resist and resent even at a very young age. The lessons are better learned through positive reinforcement, praise, and encouragement.

Read this story about Emily's day out and about with her mother and use it as an opportunity to talk with your toddlers about all these and other important out-and-about manners. Then go out and about with your toddler. Meet new people. Visit new places. And have a wonderful day with your child.

Happy travels!
— Cindy and Peggy

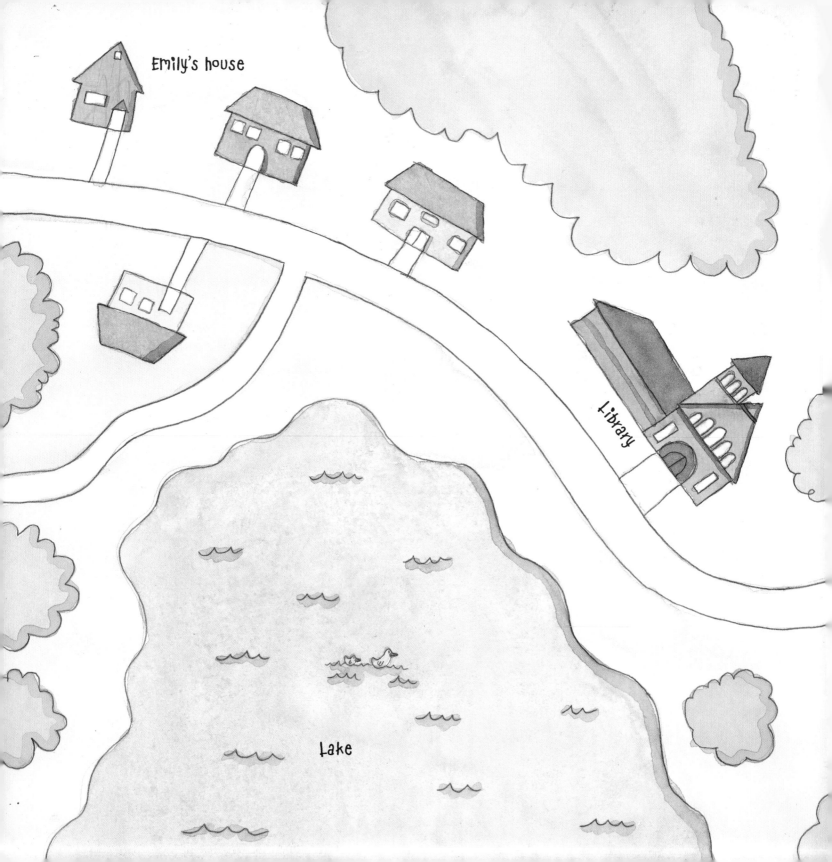